ZIONISM DECODED

IN 101 QUOTES

“Yakov Rabkin is our greatest guide to a fundamental and sad truth: Zionism is not Judaism and in many ways is the opposite of the Jewish tradition and faith. This short and piercing book shows that Zionists consciously aimed to break from the Jewish tradition and to create a new identity. Sadly, that identity has become malignant in its racism, hatred, and murderous violence towards the Palestinian people. This book helps us to understand this tragic reality, and through that understanding, to have a chance of redemption towards peace and justice.” **Jeffrey Sachs**, Professor at Columbia University

“The most concise and incisive challenge Zionist propaganda and Israeli Hasbara will ever face. With the help of 101 quotes, Rabkin exposes the huge project of historical and moral fabrication that cost the lives of so many people, Arabs and Jews alike. A must read and invaluable companion for both novices and well-read audiences on the topic of Zionism and Palestine.” **Ilan Pappé**, historian, University of Exeter, author of *Ten Myths about Israel*

“Zionism's relation to Judaism—that is, to Jewish histories and traditions—remains one of the most challenging questions posed to Judaism itself. *This book shows that Yakov Rabkin's remains one of the best-informed Jewish critics of Zionism.*” **Yaacov Yadgar**, Professor of Israel Studies, University of Oxford, author of To Be a Jewish State

“I have always admired the formidable Jewish intellectual tradition of pursuing the truth and speaking it even when to do so is to risk ostracism. Professor Rabkin exemplifies this tradition and does so with uncommon erudition.” **U.S. Ambassador Chas Freeman (ret.)**

ZIONISM DECODED

IN 101 QUOTES

Yakov Rabkin

TRACTION

Montréal

ISBN paper 978-1-77186-412-1 | ePub 978-1-77186-419-0 | PDF 978-1-77186-420-6

Cover by Leila Marshy
Book Design by Folio infographie
Editing: Robin Philpot
Proofreading: Rachel Hewitt, Shanti Maharaj

Legal Deposit, 1st quarter 2026
Bibliothèque et Archives nationales du Québec
Library and Archives Canada

Published by Baraka Books of Montreal

TRADE DISTRIBUTION & RETURNS

Canada
UTPdistribution.com

United States
Independent Publishers Group: IPGbook.com

We acknowledge the support from the Société de développement des entreprises culturelles (SODEC) and the Government of Quebec tax credit for book publishing administered by SODEC.

SODEC
Québec

TABLE OF CONTENTS

FOREWORD

They say that dynamite comes in small packages.

This compact book, more an illuminating essay with remarkable quotes, strikes Zionist fabrications between the eyes like a slingshot. And the ogre crumbles. These words come from both sides of the barricades. Sticks and stones may do the damage, so it is said, "but names will never hurt me." These do, through concise quotes, strung together like cat's eyes embedded in the road, reflecting light back to its source. Collected in apt categories, and clearly not cherry-picked, they bury the Zionist narrative.

This is a masterpiece, for Rabkin is a genius in the art of compressed, but easily read, explanation. The selection is so relevant to the clash of ideas, that the mind is engrossed into deeper comprehension of a genocidal project decades in gestations of cruelty and extremism. The book exposes layers of meaning long after the reader will have turned the last quote over and over in the mind.

There are quotes that appear to turn accepted views on their head, such as David Ben-Gurion's recognition of the Hebrew origin of indigenous Palestinians: "The agricultural community that the Arabs found in Eretz Israel in the 7th century was none other than the Hebrew farmers that remained on their land despite all the persecution and oppression of the Roman and Byzantine emperors … there is no doubt that much Jewish blood flows in their veins …" Just think who the real natives are. Those who have lived on the land for millennia, who were initially pagans turned to Judaism when it emerged five thousand years ago, converted to Christianity then Islam, or recent aliens from Brooklyn or Russia?

The quote of South Africa's Archbishop Desmond Tutu states: "In many instances [Israeli apartheid] is worse than South Africa under white minority rule."

Like South Africa, Palestine will be free, and international solidarity, combined with internal resistance can make it so.

We are presented with a brilliantly conceived literary work that traces the degeneration of Zionist Israel today, an ethnic nationalist, apartheid, settler colonial, militarized monster, at the peak of its genocidal inhumane ferocity. The monster and its allies are rent with contradictions and can be stopped by the forces of a just cause. The world must stand with Palestine.

Ronnie Kasrils
Former senior member of the African National Congress, Minister of Defense (1994–1999) and Minister of Intelligence Services (2004–2008). Johannesburg, South Africa, October 2025

INTRODUCTION

Zionism is a concept and a phenomenon that confuses many. Some view it as a natural sequel of Judaism, others as another form of antisemitism, still others as a colonial imperialist project. Some, like President Biden, are proud to be Zionists, others, like many observant Jews in Jerusalem or Brooklyn, would take it as an insult. This book presents Zionism in 101 quotes attributed to a wide variety of personalities. Who are they?

The book begins with quotes outlining the **Origins** of the modern idea of gathering the Jews in the Holy Land. These quotes come mostly from theologians, some of them famous, such as Isaac Newton. **Precursors** are Jewish intellectuals, most of them alienated from religion, who articulated ideas that can be termed as Zionist *avant la lettre.* Just as early, one could hear **Warnings** about pitfalls of concentrating large numbers of Jews in Palestine and transforming the essentially religious Jewish identity into a secular national one modelled after Central and Eastern European nations. These admonitions did not deter fervent **Ideologues** from coming up with exciting radical ideas of building a new man and a new society free from the yoke of two millennia of history. Practical colonization of Palestine took **Builders**, those who dealt with political, social and economic issues. No less important were challenges of conquering the land, a task that required the emergence of **Warriors** who used modern warfare and no-less-modern political terrorism in pursuit of Zionist goals. Zionist colonization naturally produced **Victims**. Like other colonial projects, it dispossessed and oppressed the indigenous population. But it also produced other kinds of victims, ranging from deeply religious Jews long established in Palestine to Arab Jews uprooted from their homelands to ensure the Zionists' demographic dominance. Long before it constructed a state, Zionism produced **Politicians**, many of them originating in the Russian Empire. Their plans and actions continue to shape Israel's policies and its evolving political ethos. The very establishment and continuing existence of the Zionist state has heavily depended on foreign **Supporters**, including—but not limited to—an extensive Israel Lobby consisting mostly of Jews and Evangelical Christians. From its beginnings, Zionism provoked opposition on the part of the majority of Jews. **Critics** include religious Jews rejecting the very idea of a secular state in the Holy Land, Jews who feel they believe in their homeland rather than to a distant ethno-state that claims to be Jewish, and left-wing Jews who consider Zionism a reactionary nationalist creed and an imperialist colonial project.

ORIGINS

Zionism is one of the more recent ideologies that set out to transform society. Zionists, and the State of Israel they created, represent a revolution in Jewish history, a revolution that began with the emancipation and the secularization of the Jews of Europe. Like all revolutions, Zionism was inspired by ideas. These ideas were first articulated by Protestant theologians at the turn of the 17th century and remained exclusively in the domain of Christian thinkers, activists and politicians for the first three hundred years.

The earliest book to propose a Restoration of the Jews to Palestine was published by an Anglican priest, **Francis Kett** (1547–1589), in 1585. To speed up the second coming of Christ, it posited the centrality of "ingathering of the Hebrews" as a means of fulfilling biblical prophecies. For proposing "the notion of Jewish national return to Palestine," a heresy at the time, he was promptly burned at the stake.[1]

Famous scientists, such as **Joseph Priestley** (1733–1804) and **Isaac Newton** (1643–1727) held religious beliefs envisaging an imminent "Jewish return to the Holy Land." According to Newton,

> Tis said that they who sleep in the dust shall rise again some to reward and some to punishment and Daniel himself in person is named for one of those who shall then rise again. At that time is also predicted the end of the King of the North, the fall of the great apostasy, the return of the Jewish captivity and the great tribulation.[2]

Like most Christian Zionists, Newton also believed in the conversion of the Jews to Christianity.

One of the most famous Jewish converts to Christianity, British Prime Minister **Benjamin Disraeli, Earl of Beaconsfield,** (1804–1881), wrote "an inspiring and romantic proto-Zionist saga of a man who would fire the imagination of a people."[3] While he certainly did not affect his Jewish contemporaries, his contribution was hailed later by Zionist ideologues in search of impressive precursors. Disraeli is also credited with almost singlehandedly inventing the lexicon of modern racial antisemitism. One of his admirers was **Adolf Hitler** (1889–1945), who in a 1941 speech said, "The British Jew, Lord Disraeli, once said that the racial problem was the key to world history. We National Socialists have grown up with this idea."[4] This is one of many instances of the antisemites' appreciation of Zionism.

The 1800s marks a high point in Christian Zionism. The merging of religious and political motivations of this British proto-Zionist commitment were embodied in the activities of **Lord Shaftesbury** (Anthony Ashley Cooper; 1801–1885). Epitomizing Victorian Protestant imperialism, Shaftesbury also became Chairman of the London Society for Promoting Christianity Amongst the Jews. On November 4, 1840, he placed "a memorandum to the Protestant monarchs" of Europe in *The Times of London* encouraging them to promote the Restoration of the Jews. Shaftesbury coined an important motto later taken up by promoters of Zionism: "a country without a nation in need of a nation without a country."[5] (Some attribute the sentence to Scottish clergyman Alexander Keith who visited Palestine in 1839.)

Shaftesbury strongly influenced **Henry John Temple, Viscount Palmerston** (1784–1865), British Foreign Secretary. Even though neither he nor Shaftesbury had ever consulted Jews in London or elsewhere, Palmerston wrote that,

> There exists at the present time among the Jews dispersed over Europe, a strong notion that the time is approaching when their nation is to return to Palestine ... It would be of manifest importance to the Sultan to encourage the Jews to return and to settle in Palestine because the wealth which they would bring with them would increase the resources of the Sultan's dominions.[6]

But it was **William Hechler** (1845–1931), the Anglican chaplain of the British Embassy in Vienna, who contributed most to spreading Zionism among Jews. He encouraged Theodor Herzl, more conversant with Christian than Judaic concepts, to embark on the ingathering of Jews in Palestine and introduced him to powerful rulers of Europe. In turn, Herzl invited Hechler as a non-voting delegate to the first Zionist congress in 1897, introducing him as "the first Christian Zionist."[7]

PRECURSORS

Secularization and the intellectual ferment of mid-19th-century Europe produced several Jewish authors who "nationalized" Jewish identity and envisaged a national future for the Jews. In other words, a national community had to be imagined and constituted, in this case more than in many others. Political activism in search of collective solutions was in the air. Some were nationalist, others looked for liberation in unity of the working class of different nations. Zionism was conceived by Europeans for Europeans, and the best way to understand it is in the context of Europe's political history.

According to American political scientist Benedict Anderson (1936-2015), a nation is a socially constructed community imagined by people who perceive themselves as part of it.[1] For Czech-English philosopher and anthropologist Ernest Gellner (1925-1995), nationalism is not an "awakening" (a favourite term of nationalists themselves) and self-affirmation of mythical, natural and predetermined communities.[2] Rather, it is a process of forming new communities that correspond to contemporary conditions, "while using the cultural, historical and other heritage of the pre-nationalist world as raw material." Both books were originally published in 1983. *The Invention of Tradition*, edited by Eric Hobsbawm (1917–2012) and Terence Ranger (1929–2015) appeared in the same year.[3] It shows that many traditions that seem old or claim to be so are often of recent origin and frequently invented. Interestingly, all these scholars were born in one country but worked elsewhere, which sharpened their perception of nationalism and at the same time allowed them to view this phenomenon with a degree of detachment.

Two decades later, these ideas were applied by Israeli historian Shlomo Sand (born 1946) to the Jews and the Land of Israel.[4] He showed that Zionists had to imagine a national community to a greater extent than in many other cases, where a nation had to be formed from people living in the same territory and speaking the same language. The Jews did not have any of this. Moreover, they had to be torn away from their native lands and resettled in an imaginary "historical homeland"

Moses Hess (1812–1875) was a German intellectual of Jewish descent and an early socialist. Son of an ordained rabbi, Hess showed no interest in Judaism and married a poor Catholic seamstress "in order to redress the injustice perpetrated by society." He contributed to the transformation of Judaism into a nationalist ideology by his book *Rome and Jerusalem*. Inspired by the Italian Risorgimento, he wrote:

> With the liberation of the Eternal City on the banks of the Tiber, begins the liberation of the Eternal City on the Moriah; with the renaissance of Italy heralds the rise of Judah. Jerusalem's orphaned children will also be able to participate in the great regeneration of nations.[5]

Jewish nationalism was a relatively late upshot of the *printemps des peuples* that swept over Europe in the 19th century. It affected not only those who, like Hess, abandoned Judaism but also some prominent rabbis such as **Zvi Hirsch Kalischer,** (1795–1874), born in Prussian-ruled Poland. He declared in 1862 that messianic redemption would begin with a concerted effort to re-establish the Land of Israel as the national home of the Jews:

> Why do the people of Italy and of other countries sacrifice their lives for the land of their fathers, while

we, like men bereft of strength and courage, do nothing! Are we inferior to all other peoples, who have no regard for life and fortune as compared with the love of their land and nation? Let us take to heart the examples of the Italians, Poles, and Hungarians, who laid down their lives and possessions in the struggles for national independence, while we, the children of Israel, who have the most glorious and holiest of lands as our inheritance, are spiritless and silent. Should we not be ashamed of ourselves?[6]

Another rabbinical precursor of Zionism, **Yehuda Alkalai** (1798–1878), was born in Ottoman Sarajevo. He took an interest in settlement in the Holy Land but was aware of difficulties that Jewish nationalism faces: "We are, alas, so scattered and divided today, because each Jewish community speaks a different language and had different customs. These divisions are an obstacle to the Redemption."[7]

For both rabbis, Kalischer and Alkalai, the use of force remained a foreign concept. They continued to invoke the Talmudic oath not to "rebel against the nations" (Babylonian Talmud, Ketubot, 111a) and insisted that the return to Israel would by no means involve military force: "and no sword shall cross your land" (Leviticus 26:6).

Heinrich Graetz (1817–1891) was a German Jewish historian and exegete, who pioneered a global approach to the history of the Jews. This led him to write an 11-volume *History of the Jews* which was severely criticized by his former teacher **Rabbi Samson Raphael Hirsch** (see *infra*). Graetz turned history into the faith of Jews estranged from religion: "For the first time, history, not a sacred text, becomes the arbiter of Judaism." Graetz reconceptualized Judaism as "thoroughly national" "(*Durch und durch nationell*)"[8] and therefore prepared the ground for planting Zionism among Jews.

The Odessa-based **Peretz (Pyotr) Smolenskin** (1842–1885) puts his faith in the emotion, in the vestige of Jewish soul, a *pintele yid*, as the Yiddish expression goes:

> For four thousand years we have been brothers and children of one people ... Such unity can come only from a fraternal feeling, from a national sentiment which makes everyone born a Jew declare: I am a son of this people ... No matter what his sins against religion, every Jew belongs to his people so long as he does not betray it—this is the principle we must succeed in establishing.[9]

Leo Pinsker (1821–1891) was another Russian intellectual drawn to the cosmopolitan Odessa (Russian Empire). He authored *Auto-Emancipation* in 1882 where he reiterates the regret, common in

Zionist writings, that most Jews do not see themselves as a separate nation: "In the Diaspora we maintained our individual life, and proved our power of resistance, but we lost the common bond of our national consciousness."[10] This disappointment is typical of nationalists eager to implant their nationalist ideology in an indifferent and reluctant people. Canadian-Ukrainian activist Chrystia Freeland, later promoted to Canada's Deputy Prime Minister, expressed similar disillusionment when she first visited Soviet Ukraine in the late 1980s.[11]

According to Israeli political scientist **Ze'ev Sternhell** (1935–2020), for the founders of Zionism "acceptance of the liberal concept of society would mean the end of the Jewish people as an autonomous unit."[12] Moreover, open societies pose a potent threat to the Zionist enterprise, which thrives on antisemitism.

WARNINGS

Samson Raphael Hirsch (1808–1888), a prominent rabbi, philosopher, and teacher, proposed a synthesis of Judaism and European culture and founded modern Orthodoxy in Germany. Asked to support the first proto-Zionist colonies in Palestine, he categorically refused: "What they consider a great mitzvah, is in my eyes a not insignificant transgression."[1]

Rabbi **Haim Soloveitchik** (1853–1918), a renowned Talmudic scholar from the Russian Empire who, unlike Hirsch, saw the emergence of political Zionism, warned: "The Zionists do not drive away Jews from the Torah in order to get a state. They need a state in order to drive the Jews away from the Torah."[2]

These words explain the stubborn refusal of most Orthodox Jews to serve in the Israeli military. Many people wonder why they live in Israel if they reject the Zionist state and the obligations that go with it. When I conveyed this question to a well-known anti-Zionist rabbi residing in Jerusalem's Mea Shearim quarter, he answered: "We lived here under the Ottomans, we lived here under the British, and we will remain here after the Zionists."

Looming challenges did not escape the attention of those who accepted at least Cultural Zionism. One of its leading proponents, **Ahad Ha-Am**, pseudonym of Asher Hirsch Ginzberg (1856–1927), a Jew from Odessa who made his livelihood as a tea merchant, travelled to Palestine and published a sharply worded rebuke to the settlers and their supporters:

> We have to treat the local population with love and respect, justly and rightly. And what do our brethren in the Land of Israel do? Exactly the opposite. … We tend to believe that all Arabs are desert barbarians, an asinine people who do not see or understand what is going on around them. This is a cardinal mistake. … The Arabs, and especially the city dwellers, understand very well what we want and what we do in the country, but they behave as if they do not notice it. … But when the day will come in which the life of our people in the Land of Israel will develop to such a degree that they will push aside the local population by little or by much, then it will not easily give up its place.[3]

The same concern was reiterated by the future foreign minister of Israel **Moshe Sharett** (born as **Chertok** in Kherson, Russian Empire, 1894–1965) before the UN Special Committee on Palestine on July 16, 1947: "the relations of the Jews—call it what you will, Jewish State, Jewish Palestine—with the neighbouring States will primarily depend on the treatment of the Arabs by the Jews in their own State."[4] Shortly thereafter, Zionist militias began massive expulsion of native Palestinians.

In 1948, during the war triggered by the Zionists' ethnic cleansing of Palestine, **Hannah Arendt** (1906–1975), prominent Jewish intellectual who fled Nazi Germany for the United States, wrote:

> And even if the Jews were to win the war, … the "victorious" Jews would live surrounded by an entirely hostile Arab population, secluded inside ever-threatened borders, absorbed with physical self-defense. … And all this would be the fate of a nation that—no matter how many immigrants it could still absorb and how far it extended its boundaries—would still remain a very small people greatly outnumbered by hostile neighbors.[5]

Indeed, Eastern European intellectuals, who ran the Zionist movement, had little knowledge of Palestine and its inhabitants, and there were almost no Zionists among Arab Jews before the Second World War; their representation in the Zionist congresses was then less than half of one percent of the delegates. Historian **Avi Shlaim**, born in Iraq in 1945, in a remarkable memoir relates his mother's comment: "Zionism is an Ashkenazi thing."[6] Indeed, it was largely embraced and spread by Russian Jews, even to the faraway Morocco. When the news of the partition of Palestine proposed by the British Peel Commission reached Morocco, prominent Moroccan Jews and Muslims signed a strongly worded letter to the Foreign Office in London warning "of disastrous consequences that would result in undesirable troubles between Arab and Jewish elements." The letter ends with a call for "an independent Palestinian state to be governed by democratic parliamentary institutions, the only regime that can ensure both groups in Palestine equal rights in the country so dear to them."[7]

Zionist leaders have consistently rejected efforts to establish such a democratic regime. The Russian-British philosopher **Isaiah Berlin** (1909–1997) reports his meeting on board a ship with **Avraham Stern** (1907–1942), the future head of the Stern Gang (Lehi), who was travelling from Palestine to Italy to study philosophy in the early 1930s.[8] Stern, like Jabotinsky (see infra), was a talented poet who published a collection of poems in Tel Aviv in 1928. He wrote them in Russian, just as he would write in this language to his mother and his wife. The two Russian-speaking travelers struck up a conversation, and Berlin later recalled how adamantly his interlocutor insisted that he and his friends were ready to use violence to oppose any attempt to establish a representative assembly in Palestine. Stern would later interrupt his studies and use his stay in Italy to procure arms and smuggle them to Palestine. His sense of entitlement, typical of many Russian Zionists, was expressed in a letter written (this time in Hebrew) to a friend. Noticing that there was no antisemitism in Italy, he continued: "Eventually everywhere we feel like guests at most, yet in Palestine we are landlords."[9] Indeed, the landlord need not pay much attention to the natives. This episode shows how Russian Zionists in control of their colony in Palestine saw in violence the natural means of not only "dealing with the Arabs," but also scuttling democratic process that might disturb the "landlords'" political designs.

Victor Klemperer (1881–1960), German Jewish literary scholar, wrote in his secret diary kept during the Nazi years:

> To me the Zionists, who want to go back to the Jewish state of A.D. 70 (destruction of Jerusalem by Titus) are just as offensive as the Nazis. With their nosing after blood, their ancient "cultural roots," their partly canting, partly obtuse winding back of the world they are altogether a match for the National Socialists.[10]

Ethnic nationalism is, indeed, a crucial aspect of political demodernization.

Two prominent and very different faculty members of the Hebrew University in Jerusalem confirmed, at different times, this diagnosis. **Israel Shahak** (1933–2001), professor of chemistry and anti-religious human rights activist, wrote in 1974: "I am not afraid to say publicly that Israeli Jews, and with them most Jews throughout the world, are undergoing a process of Nazification."[11] **Yeshayahu Leibowitz** (1903–1994), professor of neurophysiology and several other disciplines, and an Orthodox Torah scholar declared in a 1991 speech in Haifa: "A Nazi-like mentality also exists in our country. That is a fact."[12] He specifically called settlers affiliated with National Judaism "Judeo-Nazis."

These warnings have been confirmed by events. Critics from within Israel emphasize that the support for genocide of Palestinians among Israeli Jews in the 21st century "isn't a problem of the media concealing or manipulating. It is the fruit of militaristic racist indoctrination that begins in kindergarten and continues until death. An indoctrination that needs destruction to justify the existence of Zionism."[13]

Zionism has largely become the preserve of the right wing. Hitherto-worshipped socialist Zionist ideologues such as **Ber Borochov** (1881–1917) and **Aaron David Gordon** (1856–1922), have become irrelevant and are mostly remembered in street names in Israel. Nowadays, a left-wing Zionist appears as an oxymoron. **Maxime Rodinson** (1915–2004), renowned historian and orientalist, son of Jewish refugees from the pogroms in Belarus, who were later murdered in Auschwitz, understood the apparent paradox of a socialist Israel joining the imperialists' circle:

> The element that made it possible to connect these aspirations of Jewish shopkeepers, peddlers, craftsmen, and intellectuals in Russia and elsewhere to the conceptual orbit of imperialism was one small detail that seemed to be of no importance: Palestine was inhabited by another people.[14]

In 1948, **Albert Einstein** (1879–1955) and other pre-eminent thinkers publicly condemned as fascist the right-wing Zionism of **Vladimir Jabotinsky** (see *infra*). The steady drifting of Israeli society to the right suggests that all political Zionism, not just Jabotinsky's ideas, contains seeds of fascism, which may take time to sprout. In 2025, the veteran columnist **Gideon Levy** (born in 1953) concluded in the Israeli daily *Haaretz*, "It is no longer possible to be a Zionist and not a fascist."[15]

IDEOLOGUES

Zionism emerged from intense ideological debates that animated initially small and disparate groups of secularized Jews in Eastern and Central Europe. Most were concerned with the growth of antisemitism, a racialist creed that came to supplant the Christian Judeophobia in the 19th century. The principal ideologue and leader of the Zionist movement, **Theodor Herzl** (1860–1904), made a revealing entry in his diary:

> I achieved a freer attitude to antisemitism, which I now began to understand historically, and to pardon. Above all, I recognized the emptiness and futility of trying to "combat" antisemitism.[1]

Moreover, **Herzl** recognized that antisemitism would be harnessed to Zionist purposes since both wanted to rid Europe of its Jews. "The antisemites will become our most loyal friends, the antisemite nations will become our allies."[2]

Zionism's foundational paradox—a movement that invoked Jewish collective memory while rejecting its theological framework—was one of the reasons the majority of Jews rejected Zionism. The first Zionist Congress had to be moved from Germany to Switzerland at the request of German Jewish organizations. Thus, the national organization of German rabbis condemned the Zionists, who were then preparing for their first congress:

> The efforts of the so-called Zionists to establish a Jewish national state in the Land of Israel ... [are in conflict with] the messianic goals of Judaism, as these are expressed in the Scriptures and in other religious sources.[3]

One of the earliest Jewish ideologues of Zionism was **Eliezer Ben-Yehuda**, (1858–1922), born Leizer Itzhok Perlman in Lithuania (Russian Empire). By rejecting his original name, he inaugurated the trend which became dominant in Israel to change non-Hebrew surnames into Hebrew ones. For several decades, this was obligatory for those joining military and civil service.

Once settled in Jerusalem in 1881, he dedicated his life to the invention of the modern Hebrew language. Reacting to the mass abandonment of Judaism, he sought salvation in nationalism:

> We will be able to revive the Hebrew tongue only in a country in which the number of Hebrew inhabitants exceeds the number of gentiles. There, let us increase the number of Jews in our desolate land: let the remnants of our people return to the land of their fathers; let us revive the nation and its tongue will be revived, too! … we must make it the tongue of our children, on the soil on which it once blossomed and bore ripe fruit.[4]

However vital, Ben-Yehuda's project was put into perspective by another ideologue from Russia, who argued that it was more important to fight.

This was **Vladimir (Ze'ev) Jabotinsky** (1880–1940), whose militant ideas, albeit further radicalized by his ideological heirs, continue to shape Israel. He was born in Odessa where he attended a private Hebrew school which, according to Israeli scholar **Shlomo Avineri** (1933–2023),

> […] had no internal connection with Judaism except through the study of Hebrew … He did not recall anything Jewish there, be it Jewish history or prayers. … Anyone who goes carefully through the twenty volumes of his collected works will learn more about Russian, Italian, German, and even Ukrainian culture than about Jewish culture.[5]

This estrangement from Jewish culture, and a fortiori from Judaism, was typical of the intellectuals who built the Zionist state. The Rehovot museum of **Chaim Weizmann**, (1874-1952), born in Motal, Russian Empire, the first president of Israel, preserves his extensive library, in which books on Jewish themes and in Jewish languages constitute a miniscule part.

Jabotinsky first encountered Zionism in socialist garb during his studies in Switzerland, where many Russian Jews flocked because of the limitations of access to Russian universities. It is there that he gave his first speech:

> I spoke in Russian, in the following vein: I do not know if am a socialist, since I have not yet acquainted myself with that doctrine, but I have no doubt that I am a Zionist, because the Jewish people is a very nasty people, and its neighbours hate it, and they are right. Its end in the Diaspora will be a general Bartholomew Night, and the only rescue is general immigration to Palestine.[6]

In a 1910 essay, characteristically titled "*Homo homini lupus*" (Man Is Wolf to Man), he expressed a political philosophy that one can recognize in Israel's behaviour, including its genocide in Gaza:

> Sometimes we base too many rosy hopes on the fallacy that a certain people has itself suffered and will therefore feel the agony of another people and understand it and its conscience will not allow it to

> inflict on the weaker people what had been earlier inflicted on it. But in reality it appears that these are mere pretty phrases ... Only the Bible says "you shall not oppress a stranger; for you know the heart of the stranger, seeing you were strangers in the land of Egypt." Contemporary morality has no place for such childish humanism.[7]

Rabbi Abraham Isaac HaCohen Kook (1865–1935), born in the Russian Empire, was an unconventional thinker whose ideas, often expressed poetically, continue to be researched and interpreted. He is usually seen as the inspiration of National Judaism (*dati-leumi*), a relatively new form of Judaism that has taken root in Israel. For many of its followers, the new creed defuses moral qualms and gives religious justification to their Zionist commitment. Yet, he did not envisage a particularistic, ethnocentric redemption: "All the civilizations of the world will be renewed by the renaissance of our spirit."[8] Unlike those who claim to be his followers among the militant settlers, he saw a positive aspect of the Jews' collective powerlessness:

> External forces compelled us to leave the political arena of the world, but our withdrawal was also motivated by an internal will, as if to say that we were awaiting the advent of a happier time, when

government could be conducted without ruthlessness and barbarism.[9]

It was his son, **Rabbi Zvi Yehuda Kook** (1891–1982), who turned his father's universalist and pacifist vision into a militant creed. It is this ideology that largely inspired settlement on the lands that Israel conquered in 1967. His was always a maximalist program. Kook Jr. recalled his reaction to the November 1947 UN recommendation to partition Palestine:

> On the night when news of the United Nations decision in favour of the resurrection of the State of Israel reached us, when the people streamed into the streets to celebrate and rejoice, I could not go out and join in the jubilation. I sat alone and silent; a burden lay upon me. During those first hours I could not resign myself to what had been done. I could not accept the fact that indeed "they have … divided My land." (Joel 4:2)! Yes, where is our Hebron—have we forgotten her?! Where is our Shechem? Our Jericho? Where? Have we forgotten them? And what about all the land beyond the Jordan—each and every clod of earth, every region, hill, valley, every plot of land, that is part of the Land of Israel? Have we the right to give up even one grain of the Land of God?[10]

His disciples raised on the ideology of National Judaism continue to be the main aggressive motive force of Zionist colonization and relentless self-righteous oppression of the Palestinians.

Well before the Hamas attack of October 2023, which inflamed hatred of the Palestinians and led to the murder of thousands of babies and children in Gaza, a book written by **Rabbi Yitzhak Shapira** and **Rabbi Yosef Elitzur**, affiliated with National Judaism, argued that "it is reasonable to harm children if it is clear they will grow up to harm us. Under such circumstances they should be the ones targeted."[11] What appeared as religious extremism at first, is part of the mainstream at the time of this writing. In May 2025, former Likud parliamentarian **Moshe Feiglin,** a secular libertarian, told Israeli TV Channel 14 in the context of the genocide in Gaza, "The enemy is not Hamas, nor is it the military wing of Hamas … Every child in Gaza is the enemy."[12] This ideologue spelled out a sentiment that explains the behaviour of many IDF soldiers and is widely spread in Israeli society.

BUILDERS

Zionism has been not only an ideology but a practical political, economic colonization and relentless self-righteous oppression of the Palestinians, a project which includes social engineering, eugenics and education. While Zionist settlers began to stream to Palestine in the late 19th century, the first political building block in the Zionist project was the Balfour Declaration. In fact, it was no more than a brief letter written on November 2, 1917, by Foreign Secretary Arthur Balfour:

> His Majesty's Government view with favour the establishment in Palestine of a national home for the Jewish people, and will use their best endeavours to facilitate the achievement of this object, it being clearly understood that nothing shall be done which may prejudice the civil and religious rights of existing non-Jewish communities in Palestine, or the rights and political status enjoyed by Jews in any other country.[1]

The letter was addressed to Lord Rothschild, a leader of Britain's Jewish community, less than four percent of whose members belonged then to the Zionist movement.

Moreover, the term "national home of the Jewish people" was deliberately vague and had no precedent in international law. The letter did not delimit the territory in question, and more than a century later no Israeli government has so far defined the "defensible borders" that Israel demands. It remains an ever-expanding state without borders. On August 11, 1919, Balfour wrote:

> Zionism, be it right or wrong, good or bad, is rooted in age-long traditions, in present needs and future hopes, of far profounder import than the desires and prejudices of the 700,000 Arabs who now inhabit that ancient land.[2]

Arthur Ruppin (1876–1943) was a German Jew who headed the Palestine office of the Zionist Organisation in Jaffa and was one of the founders of Tel Aviv. Eventually he realized that "on every site where we purchase land and settle people, the present cultivators will inevitably be dispossessed." When he asked the future president of Israel **Chaim Weizmann** about the fate of these indigenous Palestinian Arabs, Weizmann replied:

"The British told us that there are there some hundred thousand niggers [Hebrew: *kushim*, negroes] and for those there is no value."[3] This is how racist duplicity became the cornerstone in the Zionist edifice in Palestine.

The task of practical development of a separate colony in Palestine was largely directed by **David Ben-Gurion** (1886–1973), born as David Grün in the Russian Empire whence, the reader must have realised by now, stem most Zionist leaders. He became Israel's first Prime Minister in 1948. Socialist by persuasion he initially did not dismiss local Arab population as transient dwellers. He even recognized their Hebrew origin:

> The agricultural community that the Arabs found in Eretz Israel in the 7th century was none other than the Hebrew farmers that remained on their land despite all the persecution and oppression of the Roman and Byzantine emperors. ... The greater majority and main structures of the Muslim falahin in western Eretz Israel present to us one racial strand and a whole ethnic unit, and there is no doubt that much Jewish blood flows in their veins—the blood of those Jewish farmers, "lay persons," who chose in the travesty of times to abandon their faith in order to remain on their land.[4]

This early belief did not prevent him from expelling these very *falahin* to clear space for European settlers.

Like in many radical European movements of his time, commitment to the collective cause was paramount. **Ben-Gurion's** focus on establishing a Zionist state overruled humanitarian concerns. In 1938, following the *Kristallnacht*, which unleashed physical violence against the Jews of Germany, Ben-Gurion said:

> If I knew that it was possible to save all the children of Germany *by transporting them to* England, and only half by transferring them to the Land of Israel, I would choose the latter, for before us lies not only the numbers of these children but the historical reckoning of the people of Israel.[5]

Unlike legitimation attempts that are made nowadays to present Israel as part of the Jewish continuity, **Ben-Gurion** emphasized that,

> Zionism in its essence is a revolutionary movement. … The very essence of Zionist thinking about the life of the Jewish people and on Hebrew history is basically revolutionary—it is a revolt against a tradition of many centuries, helplessly longing for redemption."[6]

The expulsion of Palestinian Arabs has been the consistent goal of the Zionist movement. Mass ethnic cleansing (Palestinians call it *Nakba*, catastrophe) began in 1947 and continues to this day. Zionist leader and Nakba architect **Yosef Weitz** (1890–1972) born in the Russian Empire wrote in 1940:

> It must be clear that there is no room in the country for both peoples. … If the Arabs leave it, the country will become wide and spacious for us. … The only solution is a Land of Israel … without Arabs. … Not one village must be left, not one tribe.[7]

Much of the ongoing dispossession of Palestinians has been the work of discreet bureaucrats like Weitz, a senior official in the Jewish National Fund, who supervised afforestation of the ruins of hundreds of Palestinian villages destroyed by Zionist warriors.

WARRIORS

Bureaucrats could only take charge after nearly 800,000 Palestinians had been violently expelled, subdued or killed. Zionists knew all along from the experience of European colonial powers that their settlement would not happen peacefully. "Universal brotherhood is not even a beautiful dream. Antagonism is essential to man's greatest efforts," wrote **Herzl** in 1896 in the conclusion to his foundational work, *Der Judenstaat*.

Jabotinsky sought to establish a Jewish state on both sides of the Jordan, the slogan that continues to be the official motto of the paramilitary movement Betar he founded in Riga in 1923. Jabotinsky wrote a song for Betar, which became a favourite with right-wing Zionists:

> Two banks has the Jordan—this is ours, that is too. If my land has become poor and small, it is mine from its head to its end, stretching from the sea to the wilderness, and the Jordan, the Jordan in the middle.[1]

The idea of Greater Israel applied to the West Bank by successive Israeli governments since 1967 would appear modest in comparison.

Known as the founder and theoretician of Revisionist Zionism, **Jabotinsky** was also the author of several plays and historical novels, which often drew on his literal, as opposed to rabbinic or traditional, reading of Jewish lore. One of his plays is about Samson, who, having been blinded, kills himself and brings down his enemies in death along with him (Judges 13–16). In the Zionist state that Jabotinsky did not live to see, the Samson Option articulates Israel's deterrence strategy of massive retaliation with nuclear weapons as the last resort.

He had no illusions about the attitudes of the colonized. In one of his most cited articles written and published in Russian in Berlin in 1923, he states:

> We must either suspend our settlement efforts or continue them without paying attention to the mood of the natives. Settlement can thus develop under the protection of a force that is not dependent on the local population, behind an iron wall which they will be powerless to break down.[2]

Yosef Brenner (1881–1921), poet and the son of a pious Russian Jewish family, radically transformed the best-known verse of the Jewish prayer book "Hear, O Israel, God is your Lord, God is one!" which is one of the first verses taught to children and the last to be uttered by a Jew before his death. Brenner's revised verse proclaimed: "Hear, O Israel! Not an eye for an eye. Two eyes for one eye, all their teeth for every humiliation!" He was to die a violent death in a conflict with Arabs in Jaffa.

Another early Zionist hero is **Joseph Trumpeldor** (1880–1920). A veteran of the Russo-Japanese War, he is the incarnation of romantic valour in the Zionist curriculum. Killed in a skirmish with the local Arab population, he allegedly managed to mouth the last words: "How good it is to die for the motherland." The phrase was to become, alongside the officers' oath at Masada, where, according to Flavius Josephus, about a thousand besieged anti-Roman rebels committed suicide in the year 73 CE, one of the symbols of the new determination to take up arms.

The example of **Trumpeldor**, who had been decorated by the tsar for his bravery in battle, inspired Zionist youth throughout the former Russian Empire. Students from Riga had originally encouraged **Jabotinsky**, in 1923, to set up a Zionist activist organization that took the name *Brit Yosef*

Trumpeldor (the Josef Trumpeldor Alliance), known by its acronym Betar. The organization quickly developed a strong military component. In the words of its founder, Betar is,

> [...] structured around the principle of discipline. Its aim is to turn Betar into such a world organism that would be able, at a command from the centre, to carry out at the same moment, through the scores of its limbs, the same action in every city and every state.[3]

Betar continues to be active around the world, recently involved in attacking and spying on pro-Palestinian activists and supplying their personal data to the authorities in the US and in Europe. **Albert Einstein** was among the Jewish humanists who denounced Betar in 1935, describing it as being, "as much of a danger to our youth as Hitlerism is to German youth."[4]

The earliest settlers had projected onto Palestinian reality the memories of bygone Europe: the Arab threat was often likened to the murderous shadow of the pogroms. Moreover, their actions were like those of all settler groups in a foreign territory: they took up arms to defend their settlements. Within a single century, the repugnance felt by Jews toward violence had been transformed into defiant militarism, rather than a temporary concession to the imperatives of self-defence. One of the best-known Israeli generals, **Ariel Sharon (Scheinerman**, 1928–2014), born to a Russian-Jewish family in Palestine, was an intrepid warrior. He was no less bold with respect to colonization of the occupied territories. Addressing young Zionists eager to expand Israel's borders: "Everybody has to move; run and grab as many hilltops as you can to enlarge the settlements, because everything we take now will stay ours. Everything we don't grab will go to them."[5]

Another popular military leader, **Moshe Dayan** (1915–1981), was born in the first kibbutz in Palestine also to Russian Jewish parents. Referring to the IDF —Israel Defense Force—a few months before the Six-Day War Israel would initiate and win, Dayan said:

> The Israeli army is called a "defense force" but it is not a defensive army. ... The Sinai campaign (1956), the reprisal acts and the raids across the border were purely offensive operations, and were of decisive value. ... Not only the actions which were actually carried out but also the IDF's prevailing conception is offensive ... the IDF is a characteristically offensive army as regards theory, planning and execution, in body and spirit.[6]

Contrary to the prevailing self-pity and indignation that followed the Hamas attack from Gaza in

October 2023, **Dayan** understood the predicament of the Palestinians. Speaking at the funeral of an Israeli killed by a Palestinian from Gaza in 1956, he said:

> Let us not today cast blame on the murderers. Who are we to argue against their potent hatred for us? For eight years they have been sitting in the refugee camps in Gaza, and before their eyes we have been turning the land and villages in which they and their forefathers lived into our own inheritance ...[7]

Dayan, in one of his brutally honest moments, confessed that "there is not one single place built in this country that did not have a former Arab population."[8]

The 2023 attack on southern Israel unleashed an orgy of violence on the part of Israel. At the time of this writing, nearly 70,000 Palestinians, 80% of them civilians, have been reported killed in Gaza. 70 percent of the Palestinians killed in residential buildings or similar housing were women and children. Many more are being starved to death or die of lack of medicine and medical care. Weaponizing the trauma, the vast majority of Israelis support these atrocities even though sober voices are also heard: "A sane country does not wage war against civilians, does not kill babies as a pastime, and does not engage in mass population displacement," **Yair**

Golan (born in 1962), the former deputy chief of staff of the Israeli army, said in a charged interview with a local radio station.[9]

However, **Golan** is more of an exception. **Major General Giora Eiland,** former head of Israel's National Security Council, had long advocated for a massive attack on Gaza:

> One option is a massive and complex ground operation, with no regard to duration and cost, while the second option is to create conditions where life in Gaza becomes unsustainable. Israel has already begun suspending the supply of diesel, fuel, electricity, and water, as well as closing the border crossings. Yet, it remains uncertain whether these measures are enough.[10]

Both options have been implemented in the ongoing genocide.

Such appeals made by military men are supported by scholarly settler-rabbis:

> There are situations in which we would want, deliberately, to harm specifically the innocents. Their presence and their killing are actually beneficial and helpful for us. For example: harming young children of the evil king's family, though they are now innocent. Killing them helps us to hurt him so that he will stop fighting against us.[11]

VICTIMS

Victims of Zionism include both Arabs and Jews. **Avi Schlaim** wrote:

> From whatever perspective one chooses to view it, the establishment of the state of Israel in May 1948 involved a monumental injustice to the Palestinians. ... In the history of the Palestinian people, the most traumatic event is the Nakba, which is not in fact a one-off event but the ongoing process of the dispossession and displacement of Palestinian people from their homeland that continues to this day, in the unspeakable horrors being visited by the Israeli Defence Forces (IDF) on Gaza.[1]

The Palestinian leader who organized resistance to the Zionist project was **Yasser Arafat** (1929–2004), born to Palestinian parents exiled in Egypt. In a speech to the UN General Assembly in November 1974 he offered Israel peace: "Today I come bearing an olive branch in one hand, and the freedom fighter's gun in the other. Do not let the olive branch fall from my hand. I repeat, do not let the olive branch fall from my hand."[2] His pleas went largely unheeded, and Zionist encroachment on Palestinian lands continued. The first Intifada broke out in 1987 and lasted for six years. The uprising consisted mostly of acts of civil disobedience but was confronted with lethal force. It was **Yitzhak Rabin** (1922–1995) born of Russian Jewish parents, who as minister of defense ordered the army to use "Force, might and beatings."[3] In 1992, he admitted: "I would like Gaza to sink into the sea, but that won't happen, and a solution must be found."[4] International and internal pressure led Rabin to embrace peace and conclude the so-called Oslo Accords with Arafat in 1993. A short time afterwards **Rabin** was assassinated by a follower of National Judaism, and the way to peace was blocked. **Gideon Levy**, one of Israel's intrepid reporters covering the Palestinians, lamented over twenty years later:

> What good have all of Arafat's compromises done for the Palestinian people? What came out of the recognition of Israel, of the settling for a Palestinian state on 22 percent of the territory, of the negotiations with Zionism and the United States? Nothing but the entrenchment of the Israeli occupation and the strengthening and massive development of the settlement project.[5]

Edward Said (1935–2003), prominent Palestinian-American scholar and public intellectual, was sceptical of the Oslo Accords from the beginning:

> The fashion-show vulgarities of the White House ceremony, the degrading spectacle of Yasser Arafat thanking everyone for the suspension of most of his people's rights, and the fatuous solemnity of Bill Clinton's performance, like a 20th-century Roman emperor shepherding two vassal kings through rituals of reconciliation and obeisance: all these only temporarily obscure the truly astonishing proportions of the Palestinian capitulation.[6]

The "Gaza Peace Summit" presided by President Trump with thirty Arab and European officials duly in attendance on October 13, 2025, would be even more grotesque as no Gazans or Israelis took part in the show. The deep imbalance of forces between Israel and the Palestinians has doomed the implementation of previous peace accords through negotiation. Israel's policy was summed up by British-Israeli historian **Avi Shlaim** with reference to continuing Zionist colonization of the West Bank, as elsewhere, in the following words: "Netanyahu is like a man who, while negotiating the division of a pizza, continues to eat it."[7]

Zionism has also gravely damaged Jews. Most Zionist founding fathers had a profound disdain for

Jews of their time, a kind of Jewish self-hate. **Herzl** had already noted in 1894 that Jews had "taken on a number of antisocial characteristics in the ghettos of Europe, and that Jewish character was damaged." **Brenner** likened Jews to "filthy dogs, inhuman, wounded dogs."[8]

Manufacturing the New Hebrew was therefore vitally important. It was particularly urgent to re-educate the traditionally religious Jews who had been uprooted from Arab countries to populate the newly created Zionist state. Israeli educators embarked on a project similar to the colonialist *mission civilisatrice* or the white man's burden. **Ella Shohat** (born in 1959) a scholar who experienced and studied the fate of the Arab Jew remarks, "The official ideology denies the Arabness of the Arab Jews."[9]

In the Knesset, Israeli parliamentarian **David-Zvi Pinkas**, Hungarian born,(1895–1952), deplored what was happening in the early 1950s in re-education camps set up for Yemenite Jewish children separated from their parents: "I see nothing in what is being done in these camps but the cultural and religious murder of the tribes of Israel."[10] For many Yemenites, the contrast with their native land could not have been starker:

> The Arabs among whom we lived did not bother us, not even in the most insignificant of our religious observances. … And here, they treat us with contempt, and force our people to profane the Sabbath. They mock us; laugh at our traditional beliefs, our prayers and the religious observances of our Holy Torah.[11]

Israeli officials also kidnapped hundreds of babies born to immigrants from Yemen in order to transform them into "true Israelis." The government assured the parents that their children had died. "The Yemenites feel this is their holocaust".[12]

POLITICIANS

Zionism is a political movement formed by groups of disparate national and ideological origins. Even though political life had begun long before the establishment of the Zionist state in 1948, contemporary politicians, mostly born in Israel, provide a better perspective on Zionism than their predecessors.

The long-serving Prime Minister **Benjamin Netanyahu** (born in 1949), who greatly solidified cooperation with the United States, once said: "I know what America is. America is a thing you can move very easily, move it in the right direction. They won't get in our way."[1] The continuing genocide in Gaza, violent dispossession of Palestinians on the rest of the occupied territories and the US involvement in the attack on Iran have so far proven him right.

A rising star on Israel's political horizon is **May Golan** (born in 1986), anti-immigration activist appointed Minister for Social Equality. She belongs to the new generation of politicians who do not beat about the bush. She declared at a public rally in 2013: "If I am racist for wanting to defend my country and for wanting to protect my basic rights and security, then I'm a proud racist."[2] A year earlier, her colleague **Miri Regev** (born in 1965), former brigadier general and IDF spokesperson, referred to Sudanese refugees in Israel as "a cancer in the nation's body" and declared that she "is proud to be a fascist."[3] She would later be appointed Minister of Culture. "They have to die and their houses should be demolished so that they cannot bear any more terrorists," said Israeli parliamentarian **Ayelet Shaked** (born in 1976) in 2014, just before she assumed the post of the Minister of Justice. She explained:

> Behind every terrorist stands dozens of men and women without whom he could not engage in terrorism. They are all enemy combatants, and their blood shall be on all their heads. Now this also includes the mothers of the martyrs, who send them to hell with flowers and kisses. They should follow their sons, nothing would be more just. They should go, as should the physical homes in which they raised the snakes. Otherwise, more little snakes will be raised there.[4]

These Israeli politicians embody an important political trend. They have long felt free of the conventions of liberal democracy and are harbingers of this trend in Western societies. "Ethnonationalist ideology grows when accountable democracy withers. Israel is the ultimate model and goal."[5] In Israel, the settler colonial nature of the Zionist state discredits democratic pretences in the country's political culture. In Europe and countries of European settlement elsewhere, it is the acute social inequality and the scapegoating of the foreign-born that has scratched the thin layer of the democratic varnish applied after the fall of Nazism. Racism that justified plundering colonies is naturally coming back.

> Gaza deserves death. The 2.6 million terrorists in Gaza deserve death! … Men, women, and children—in every way possible, we must simply carry out a Holocaust on them—yes, read that again—H-O-L-O-C-A-U-S-T! For me, gas chambers. Train cars. And other cruel forms of death for these Nazis. Without fear, without hesitation—simply crush, eradicate, slaughter, flatten, dismantle, smash, shatter … Gaza deserves death. Let there be a Holocaust in Gaza!

These are the words of **Elad Barashi**, a TV producer who spoke thus on air in February 2025.[6]

Israel has long been at the forefront of undermining public international law. Even though its legitimacy reposes partly in the November 29, 1947,

UN General Assembly resolution on the partition of Palestine, Israel has consistently ignored dozens of UN resolutions. **Ben-Gurion** used to disdain the UN ("*UNO, shmuno*") arguing at a cabinet meeting in 1955 that Israel should occupy Gaza. Israel's envoy **Gilad Menashe Erdan** (born in 1970) publicly shredded the UN Charter before the organisation's General Assembly in May 2024. He condemned as antisemites the overwhelming majority of UN.members who voted to admit Palestine as a full member.

The Israeli novelist **Amos Oz** (1939–2018) parodied this attitude:

> Our sufferings have granted us immunity papers, as it were, a moral carte blanche. After what all those dirty goyim [non-Jews] have done to us, none of them is entitled to preach morality to us. We, on the other hand, have carte blanche, because we were victims and have suffered so much. Once a victim, always a victim, and victimhood entitles its owners to a moral exemption.[7]

SUPPORTERS

Zionism has always relied on the support of different groups and countries. By far the most numerous contingent of Israel's loyal supporters are tens of millions of Christian Zionists particularly influential in the United States. Popular evangelical preacher **Jerry Falwell** (1933–2007) saw the founding of the State of Israel in 1948 as the most crucial event in history since the ascension of Jesus to heaven, and

> proof that the second coming of Jesus Christ is nigh. ... Without a State of Israel in the Holy Land, there cannot be the second coming of Jesus Christ, nor can there be a Last Judgement, nor the End of the World.[1]

This hitherto solid support from the Christian right fractured in 2025 under the impact of graphic images of the genocide in Gaza. Moreover, several of its prominent figures such as Tucker Carlson became eloquent critics of Israel and its influence on the U.S. foreign policy. Zionism took a while to become widespread among Jews. The Russian

Empire with its pogroms (mostly in what are today Ukraine and Moldova) was logically the most fertile ground for Zionist support. Christian majority countries in Europe and North America discriminated against Jews, but their social and economic progress was promising. American Jews began to embrace Zionism during the Second World War as Jews of Russian descent came to replace the old German Jewish elites who were indifferent or hostile to Zionism. The situation changed even more drastically after the Israeli victory in 1967. "In most of the Jewish world today, rejecting Jewish statehood is a greater heresy than rejecting Judaism itself. ... We have built an altar and thrown an entire [Palestinian] society on the flames," observes **Peter Beinart** (born in 1971), one of the most insightful analysts of the US Jewish community.[2] **Élie Barnavi** (born in 1946), historian and former Israeli ambassador to Paris, has long concluded that the Jewish Diaspora is "transformed into an Israeli vassal."[3]

An important tool of rallying support for Zionism is the conflation of anti-Zionism with antisemitism. This was not easy since Herzl and his followers openly sought and obtained help from antisemites in several countries including Nazi Germany. At an annual conference in Israel sponsored by the

American Jewish Congress in 1972, former Israeli foreign minister **Abba Eban** (1915–2002) laid out a long-term strategy: "… the distinction between antisemitism and anti-Zionism is not a distinction at all. Anti-Zionism is merely the new antisemitism."[4] Consistently pursued, this strategy has born fruit in most Western countries. To deflect criticism of the genocide in Gaza, false accusations of antisemtisim have led to discreditation, dismissal from work, deportations and imprisonment.

A common tool of rallying Jewish support is fear mongering, and Hollywood has long been mobilized to support Israel. In response to the world-wide non-violent campaign of boycott, divestment and sanctions (BDS) against Israel, **Ryan Kavanaugh** (born in 1974), CEO of a production company responsible for financing more than 200 films, urged his colleagues to stifle all criticism of Israel: "It is our job to keep another Holocaust from happening."[5]

Crucial support for Israel comes from politicians. Thus, decades before he became a US president, **Joe Biden** (born in 1942), a young senator from Delaware, was spelling out his commitment to Israel: "Israel is 'the best $3 billion investment we make,' he declared in the Senate back in 1986. 'Were there not an Israel,' he added, 'the United States of America would have to invent an Israel to protect our interests in the region.'"[6]

Many years later, he confided in an interview:

> I got in trouble many times for saying you don't have to be a Jew to be a Zionist, and I am a Zionist. I make no apologies for that. That's a reality.... Imagine our circumstance in the world were there no Israel. How many battleships would there be? How many troops would be stationed?[7]

Benjamin Netanyahu in his post at the United Nations in New York assiduously worked to galvanize evangelical Christians' pro-Israel sentiment and make them a critical part of the Israel lobby. These efforts have paid off as Israel continues to enjoy bi-partisan support from the American ruling class. "Israel and the United States are joined at the hip,"[8] keeps repeating **John Mearsheimer** (born in 1947), co-author of *The Israel Lobby.*

The line between religious and political support is often blurred. **Mike Huckabee** (born in 1975), a Baptist minister, said during his confirmation hearing as US ambassador to Israel that the modern Zionist state has "the biblical mandate that goes all the way back to the time of Abraham, 3,500 years ago."[9]

The belief in domination and supremacy, usually presented as "Israel's right to self-defence," continues to define Israeli policies against the Palestinians, the neighbouring countries, and even against Iran, which Israel subjected to an unprovoked attack in June 2025. This act enjoyed solid support from the G7—all of which are countries with a recent history of brutal colonialism that continue to enjoy the wealth plundered from the natives. Thus, Germany's chancellor **Friedrich Merz** (born in 1955) defended Israel's attacks on Iran, saying it was "dirty work Israel is doing for all of us."[10] The outstanding impunity of the small Zionist state in West Asia has thus been assured by the consistent support, complicity and interests of Western ruling classes. This support suffers from profound democratic deficit. Most Western citizens condemn Israel, and even in the United States, popularity of Zionism is in free fall. This democratic deficit is not exceptional and can also be observed in Western governments' economic and social policies that go against public opinion.

Russia's support is more nuanced and ambivalent. It condemned the Israeli aggression on Iran in the summer of 2025, but when asked at a press conference why Moscow was not helping Tehran more, President **Vladimir Putin** (born in 1952) said: "Every conflict is rather unique. I want to draw your attention to the fact that almost two million Russian-speaking people live in Israel; it is almost a Russian-speaking country today."[11] This answer reflects the fundamentally positive public view of Israel in Russian society. Those who shape public opinion in Russia have colleagues, friends, and sometimes relatives among Russian-speaking Israelis, most of whom stem from the same urban Soviet and post-Soviet milieux. Moreover, Jewish anti-Zionist activities were discredited during the Soviet period and lack the vigour one finds among American, British and even Israeli Jews.

For **Noam Chomsky** (born in 1928), scholar of linguistics and public intellectual, "People who call themselves supporters of Israel are actually supporters of its moral degeneration and ultimate destruction."[12]

CRITICS

Zionism is a political movement that has attracted much criticism throughout its relatively short history. Its first detractors were Jews. These can be divided into three categories. The first one includes religious Jews rejecting the very idea of a Zionist state in the Holy Land. Based on a Talmudic injunction not to go to the Holy Land *en masse*, let alone to use force in doing so, their opposition has been steady since the very inception of the Zionist idea.

Rabbi Elhonan Wasserman (1875–1941), a pillar of non-Hasidic Orthodoxy, argued that "the National idea is nothing but a modern idol." Wasserman believed that the Nazi persecutions, of which he was soon to become a victim, were the direct consequence of Zionism:

> Nowadays, the Jews have chosen two "idols" to which they offer up their sacrifices. They are Socialism and Nationalism. ... These two forms of idol-worship have poisoned the minds and the hearts of Hebrew

> Youth. A miracle has happened: in Heaven these two idolatries have been merged into one—National-Socialism. There has been formed from them a fearful rod of wrath which hits at the Jews in all corners of the globe. The abominations to which we have bowed down strike back at us.[1]

Loyal to the millennial tradition of pacifism and fearing the eternal violence that a Zionist state would bring to Palestine, Rabbi **Yosef Zvi Duschinsky** (1868–1948), addressing the UN Special Committee on Palestine on behalf of Orthodox Jews in July 1947, reiterated his "definite opposition to a Jewish state in any part of Palestine."[2] While many Jews rallied to Zionism in the wake of the Six Day War, **Rabbi Yoel Teitelbaum**, the Satmar Rebbe (1887–1979), reminded his followers that the Zionists had sacrificed thousands of lives on the altar of the state that he considered to be the source of all violence in the region:

> It is clear as day that the Torah obligates us to make every effort to mediate for peace and avoid war. These evil people, the Zionists, do the opposite of the Torah view and quarrel with the nations constantly.[3]

Principled opposition to Zionism was also the hallmark of **Rabbi Israel Abuhatsera**, better known as Baba Salé (1890–1984), revered by many Sephardic

Jews. It is said that when he completed reading *Vayoel Moshe*, a scholarly anti-Zionist work written by the Satmar Rebbe, he called the author "a pillar of fire whose radiance should lead us all to the arrival of the Messiah."[4]

The opposition was not limited to Jewish Orthodoxy. Reform rabbis in the United States and Europe were equally categorical. **Kaufmann Kohler** (1843–1926), the President of the Hebrew Union College, the Reform movement's rabbinical academy in Cincinnati, Ohio, said in 1916 when Russian Jews resettled to the United States and were spreading Zionist ideas: "Ignorance and irreligion are at the bottom of the whole movement of political Zionism. A sober student of Jewish history and a genuine lover of his co-religionists sees that the Zionist agitation contradicts everything that is typical of Jews and Judaism."[5]

"Reform Judaism is spiritual, Zionism is political. The outlook of Reform Judaism is the world. The outlook of Zionism is a corner of western Asia," declared **Rabbi David Philipson** (1862–1949) in 1942[6] after the Zionist conference in the Biltmore Hotel in New York demanded the establishment of a separate Jewish state, a radical departure from the movement's previous more moderate official positions.

Jews in Iran are well aware of the difference between Judaism and Zionism. While their country is staunchly opposed to Zionism, Jewish life continues unimpeded. Thus, **Yehuda Gerami** (born in 1983), chief rabbi of Iran, reminded Israelis:

> Know that you Zionists do not represent Judaism and do not represent the Jewish people. … You only represent the idea of a political movement whose ideas and values oppose the ideas and values of our holy Torah and the Jewish religion. We strongly condemn your aggressive actions and emphasize to the whole world: There is a big difference between Judaism and Zionism.[7]

The second category of critics includes Jews who feel they belong in their homeland rather than in a distant ethno-state that claims to be Jewish. One of the first such critics was the only Jewish member of the British government who tried to prevent the issuing of the Balfour Declaration. In August 1917, **Edwin Montagu** (1879–1924) wrote prophetically:

> I wish to place on record my view that the policy of His Majesty's Government is antisemitic in result will prove a rallying ground for Antisemites in every country in the world. … Zionism has always seemed to me to be a mischievous political creed, untenable by any patriotic citizen of the United Kingdom. …

When the Jews are told that Palestine is their national home ... you will find a population in Palestine driving out its present inhabitants, taking all the best in the country ..."

Reiterating a traditional Jewish interpretation, Montagu could not hide his sarcasm:

> I certainly do not dissent from the view, commonly held, as I have always understood, by the Jews before Zionism was invented, that to bring the Jews back to form a nation in the country from which they were dispersed would require Divine leadership. I have never heard it suggested, even by their most fervent admirers, that either Mr. Balfour or Lord Rothschild would prove to be the Messiah.[8]

Uri Misgav (born in 1974), Israeli journalist and teacher, wrote in *Haaretz* during one of the military assaults on Gaza in 2014:

> In the state of the Jewish people it's already too late. There is no place where we can take the shame and the terror. The center is apathetic. The left is defeated and afraid, in despair, emigrating, fighting among itself, just as in Germany of the early 1930s. Meanwhile generations of Israelis, incited and consumed with hatred, are flooding the public space, and there is nobody to confront them.[9]

William Blum, (1933–2018) American Jewish author and journalist, debunks the Zionist idea of Israel being a redemption after the Nazi genocide: "The worst thing that ever happened to the Jewish people is the Holocaust. The second worst thing that ever happened to the Jewish people is the state of Israel."[10]

The third category of Jewish critics of Zionism are left-wing Jews who consider Zionism a reactionary nationalist creed and an imperialist colonial project. Veteran polticial activist **Moshe Machover** (born in 1937) formulated a concise progressive critique of Zionism:

> Indeed, if you believe that Jews can and should live in freedom and dignity among non-Jews in any country, that antisemitism can be fought and beaten—then you are thinking as a progressive person. But if you believe that Jews can have no place here, that they should not waste their time fighting against antisemitism, but go away "where they belong," to live "among their own kind," then you are thinking as an antisemite—or a Zionist.[11]

Nowadays, people in many countries turn away from Israel, making Western support for the Zionist state sharpen the already severe democratic deficit. Racist aspects of Israeli society immediately alert those familiar with racial exploitation. Religious and anti-apartheid leader **Archbishop Desmond Tutu** (1931–2021) said in 2002: "I believe Israel has a right to secure borders. What is not so understandable, nor justified, is what it did to another people to guarantee its existence." After visiting Israel in 2009, he concluded that "In many instances [Israeli apartheid] is worse than South Africa under white minority rule."[12] While ruling classes continue to support and arm Israel despite their own citizenry, the ruins of Gaza stand as silent witnesses to Zionist violence. In the words of the already quoted **John Mearsheimer**, a world authority in international relations, "what the Zionists and now Israel have done to the Palestinians over time is one of the greatest crimes in modern history."[13]

Some Israelis are aware of this and of the stark alternative left for Israel/Palestine. According to the Iranian-born **Orly Noy** (born in 1970), editor of the news site *Siha mekomit* (Local Call),

> The Gaza holocaust was made possible by the embrace of the ethno-supremacist logic inherent to Zionism. Therefore it must be said clearly: Zionism, in all its forms, cannot be cleansed of the stain of this crime. It must be brought to an end.

> Denazification will be long and all-encompassing, touching every aspect of our collective life. We will likely sacrifice more generations — both victims and perpetrators — before this scourge is fully uprooted. But the process must begin now, with the refusal to commit the horrors taking place daily in Gaza, and the refusal to let them pass as normal.
>
> Only two paths remain: either a Jewish, messianic, genocidal state, or a truly democratic state for all its citizens.[14]

***

The quotes presented here may help understand how Zionism—an ideology and a settlement project—has produced Israel as it is today. Proverbial arrogance and a sense of impunity help justify genocide by manipulated references to the Holocaust. Israel is a pioneer in high-tech surveillance, targeted assassinations and the applications of AI to genocidal extermination. Israel is also a pioneer in normalizing fascist discourse and behaviour in public life. Israel's hubris and chutzpah—all of which are contrary to core Jewish values—will no doubt lead this moral monster of a state straight to perdition. In the meantime, it is important to see Zionism not as a continuation of Jewish history and tradition, but, rather, as a radical colonial project.

Israel is a country without borders in more ways than one. Its leaders have never specified the defensible borders they want. Its ideology ignores borders, pretending that it is the state of the world's Jews. Misleading expressions such as "Jewish state" and "Hebrew state" have polluted the media, so much so that they have entered into everyday language. Israeli leaders ignore borders, intervening in the political process of other countries, particularly in the United States. In the Middle East, the IDF pays no heed to borders, striking targets in its neighbouring countries, interventions carried out with impunity and cooperation with Western countries. Israel, for all its embrace of technological modernity, thus remains bound by the reactionary demodernizing Zionist ideology. This is why its history should teach all of us important lessons about the pitfalls of ethnic nationalism, militarism and self-righteousness, growing dangers that have emerged in many countries.

Notes

Origins

1. Thomas D. Ice, "Lovers of Zion: A History of Christian Zionism," May 2009.
2. Yaakov Lappin, "The first Christian Zionist? Secret writings by Isaac Newton reveal his views on the Jewish return to Israel," Ynetnews.com, June 22, 2007. "See also: Stephen David Snobelen, "Isaac Newton, the Jews, and Christian Zionism," *Iyyun: The Jerusalem Philosophical Quarterly* 69 (January 2021): 17–30.
3. Eli Kavon, "Disraeli's redeemer: the rise and fall of David Alroy," *The Jerusalem Post*, August 20, 2016.
4. Quoted in: Pankaj Mishra, *The World after Gaza: A History*, London: Penguin, 2025, p. 17, footnote.
5. "Memorandum to Protestant Monarchs of Europe for the restoration of the Jews to Palestine", *The Times* (London) August 26, 1841, pp. 5-6.
6. Barbara W. Tuchman, *Bible and Sword: England and Palestine from the Bronze Age to Balfour*, New York: Ballatine Books, 1956, p. 175.
7. Claude Duvernoy, *The Prince and the Prophet*, Jerusalem : Département des publications de l'Agence juive, 1966.

Precursors

1. Benedict Anderson, *Imagined Communities: Reflections on the Origin and Spread of Nationalism*, London: Verso, 1983.
2. Ernest Gellner, *Nations and Nationalism*, Ithaca, NY: Cornell University Press, 1983.
3. Eric Hobsbawm and Terence Ranger, *The Invention of Tradition*, Cambridge: Cambridge University Press, 1983.
4. Shlomo Sand, *The Invention of the Jewish People*, London: Verso, 2009; Shlomo Sand, *The Invention of the Land of Israel: From Holy Land to Homeland*, London: Verso, 2014.
5. Moses Hess, *Rome and Jerusalem. A Study in Jewish Nationalism,* New York: Bloch Publishing Company, 1918, p. 35.
6. Shlomo Avineri, "Zionism and the Jewish Religious Tradition," in Shmuel Almog et al., eds., *Zionism and Religion*, Hanover, NH: Brandeis University Press et University Press of New England, 1998, p. 4.
7. Arthur Hertzberg, *The Zionist Idea,* New York: Atheneum, 1969, p. 105.
8. Heinrich Graetz, *The Structure of Jewish History,* New York: Jewish Theological Seminary, 1975, p. 114.
9. Hertzberg, *op. cit.*, p. 146.
10. Leo Pinsker, *Auto-Emancipation*, New York: Maccabaean Publishing Company, 1906, p. 6.
11. Chrystia Freeland, *"My Ukraine, and Putin's Big Lie,"* *Quartz*, 20 July, 2022.
12. Zeev Sternhell, *The Founding Myths of Israel*, Princeton: Princeton University Press, 1998, p. 55.

Warnings

1. *Shemesh Marpe (Iggerot u-mikhtavim),* Brooklyn, NY: Mesorah Publications, 1992, p. 215.

2. Aharon Rosenberg (ed.), *Mishkenoth haro'yim*. New York: Nechmod, 1984–1987 (3 volumes), vol. 2, p. 269.
3. Shlomo Avineri, *The Making of Modern Zionism. The Intellectual Origins of the Jewish State*. New York: Basic Books, 1981, p. 123.
4. United Nations Special Committee on Palestine (SCOP), "Question of Palestine," Verbatim record, July 16, 1947.
5. Hannah Arendt, "To Save the Jewish Homeland," in *Jew as Pariah*, New York: Grove Press, 1978, p. 187.
6. Avi Shlaim, *Three Worlds: Memoirs of an Arab-Jew*. London: OneWorld, 2023.
7. Mohammed Kenbib, *Juifs et musulmans au Maroc, 1859–1948*, Rabat : Université Mohammed V, 1994, p. 557.
8. Michael Ignatieff, *Isaiah Berlin : A Life*, Toronto: Penguin Books, 1998, p. 80.
9. "Letter Handwritten and Signed by Lehi Founder Avraham Stern ("Yair") – Florence, 1934," at https://www.kedem-auctions.com/.
10. Victor Klemperer, *I Will Bear Witness 1933-41: A Diary of the Nazi Years*, New York: Modern Library, 1999. https://www.goodreads.com/work/quotes/247288
11. Israel Shahak, "This is my Opinion", *SWASIA North Africa*, 1(48), December 27, 1974.
12. Rod Such, "Warnings of Israeli fascism should be heeded, not condemned," *The Electronic Intifada*, April 27, 2021.
13. Hanin Majadli, "Ignoring Massacres in Gaza City While Protesting for Democracy in Tel Aviv," *Haaretz*, March 21, 2025.
14. Maxime Rodinson, *Israel: A Colonial-Settler State?* New York: Monad Press, 1973, p. 38.
15. Gideon Levy, "We Israelis Are All Itamar Ben-Gvir," *Haaretz*, October 29, 2025.

Ideologues

1. *The Diaries of Theodore Herzl*, London: Gollancz, 1958, p. 6.
2. Tom Segev, *One Palestine Complete: Jews and Arabs under the British Mandate*, New York: Metropolitan Books, 2000, p. 47.
3. Aviezer Ravitzky, *Messianism, Zionism, and Jewish Religious Radicalism*, Chicago: The University of Chicago Press, 1996, p. 14.
4. Avineri, 1981, *op. cit.*, p. 85.
5. Avineri 1981, *op. cit.*, p. 160-161.
6. Avineri 1981, *op. cit.*, p. 162.
7. Avineri 1981, *op. cit.*, p. 164.
8. Avineri 1981, *op. cit.*, p. 195.
9. Avineri 1981, *op. cit.*, p. 196.
10. Raina Weinstein, "Religious Zionism: Tzvi Yehuda Kook on Redemption and the State," at tikvah.org.
11. Zvi Bar'el, "Fundamentalism into the Mainstream," *Haaretz*, August 22, 2010.
12. "'Every Baby In Gaza Is An Enemy': Ex-Israeli Lawmaker's Shocking Remarks," *NDTV*, April 22, 2025.

Builders

1. Balfour Declaration: Text of the Declaration, November 2, 1917. Jewishvirtuallibrary.org.
2. Mahmoud Abbas, "Lord Balfour's Burden," *The Cairo Review of Global Affairs*, Fall 2017; also: Avi Shlaim, *Genocide in Gaza: Israel, Hamas, and the Long War on Palestine*, Belfast: The Irish Pages Press, 2025, p. 22.
3. Yosef Heller, *Bemaavak lemedina*, Jerusalem: Merkaz Zalman Shazar, 1996, p. 140.
4. "Leverur Motsa Ha'Falahim," Luach Achiezer, New York, 1917, pp. 118-27, reprinted in *Anachnu U'Shcheneinu*, Tel Aviv:

Davar, 1931, pp. 13-25; https://en.wikiquote.org/wiki/David_Ben-Gurion.

5. Dina Porat, "Une question d'historiographie: L'attitude de Ben-Gurion à l'égard des juifs d'Europe à l'époque du génocide," in : Florence Heymann, and Michel Abitbol, eds., *L'historiographie israélienne aujourd'hui*, Paris: CNRS éditions, 1998, p. 120.
6. Avineri 1981, *op. cit.*, p. 200.
7. Benny Morris, *The Birth of the Palestinian Refugee Problem, 1947–1949*, Cambridge, Cambridge University Press, 1987, p. 27.

Warriors

1. https://www.youtube.com/watch?v=flodVOa5NBw&ab_channel=JewishSongswithTranslations
2. Ze'ev Jabotinsky, as quoted in Avi Shlaïm, *The Iron Wall: Israel and the Arab World*, New York: W. W. Norton, 2014, p. 14.
3. Avineri 1981, *op. cit.*, p. 172.
4. Joseph B. Schechtman, *Fighter and Prophet*, New York: Thomas Yoseloff, 1961, p. 261.
5. Rashid Khalidi, "No Chance of Peace With Settlements Around," *New York Times*, May 18, 2011.
6. https://en.wikiquote.org/wiki/Moshe_Dayan April 1967. This quote is the epigraph to *The Israeli Military and the Origins of the 1967 War* by Ami Gluska, New York: Routledge, 2007.
7. Mordechai Bar-On, *Moshe Dayan: Israel's Controversial Hero*, New Haven, CT: Yale University Press, 2012, p. 128-129.
8. Quoted in: Moshe Machover, "Zionism: Why We Oppose It" in: Moshe Machover and M. Jafar, *Zionism and War and Peace in the Middle East*, London: Palestine Solidarity Campaign, 1978.

9. Astha Rajvanshi, "Ex-Israeli general hits out at government for 'killing babies as a pastime' in Gaza," *NBC News*, May 20, 2025
10. Giora Eiland, "It's time to rip off the Hamas band-aid," Archive Today, Ynetnews.com, October 12, 2023.
11. Yitzhak Shapira and Yosef Elitzur, *Torat HaMelekh*, Yitzhar: Od Yosef Chai Yeshiva, 2009, p. 198.

Victims

1. Avi Shlaim, 2025, *op. cit.*, p. 243–244.
2. https://en.wikisource.org/wiki/Yasser_Arafat%27s_1974_UN_General_Assembly_speech.
3. David K. Shipler, "U.S. Jews Torn Over Arab Beatings." *The New York Times*, January 26, 1988.
4. "Middle East | Analysis: Hopeless in Gaza." *BBC News*. November 20, 2000.
5. Gideon Levy, "This Biography Makes It Clear: The Founder of the Palestinian Popular Front Was Right," *Haaretz*, April 15, 2018.
6. Edward Said, "The Morning After," *London Review of Books*, Vol. 15, No. 20, October 21, 1993.
7. Mohammed Ayoob, "Israel-Palestine negotiations: The road to nowhere," *Al Jazeera*, July 29, 2013.
8. Noah Efron, "Trembling with Fear: How Secular Israelis See the Ultra-Orthodox, and Why," *Tikkun*, vol. 6, no. 5, 1991, pp. 88–89.
9. Ella Shohat. "The Invention of the Mizrahim," *Journal of Palestine Studies*, Vol. 29, No. 1, 1999, pp. 5–20.
10. Ruth Blau, *Les gardiens de la cité,* Paris: Flammarion, 1978, p. 271.
11. *Ibid.*, p. 271.
12. Sarah Helm, "Yemeni Jews describe their holocaust: Sarah Helm in Yehud reports on claims that Israelis stole

4,500 children from immigrants," *The Independent*, April 17, 1994.

Politicians

1. As quoted in "Netanyahu: 'America is a thing you can move very easily,'" *The Washington Post*, Washington, D.C., July 16, 2010.
2. Chris McGreal, "Israel: self-proclaimed 'racist' politician nominated as New York consul general," *The Guardian*, April 20, 2023.
3. Asher Schechter, "How Likud MK Miri Regev Talked Her Way to the Top," *Haaretz*, December 21, 2012.
4. Mehmet Çelik, "Israeli MP Ayelet Shaked who called for genocide of Palestinians named Justice Minister," *Daily Sabah*, May 8, 2015.
5. Anthony Loewenstein, *The Palestine Laboratory: How Israel Exports the Technology of Occupation Around the World*, New York: Verso, 2023.
6. Arwa Mahdawi, "'Gaza must be eliminated': Israel's airwaves are filled with pro-genocide propaganda," *The Guardian*, June 27, 2025.
7. Amos Oz, *The Slopes of Lebanon*, San Diego: Harcourt, Brace Jovanovich, 1989, p. 40.

Supporters

1. Rodrigue Tremblay, *Pourquoi Bush veut la guerre*, Montreal: Les Intouchables, 2003, p. 118.
2. Peter Beinart, *Being Jewish After the Destruction of Gaza*, New York: Alfred A. Knopf, 2025, p. 102.
3. Élie Barnavi, "Sionismes," in Élie Barnavi and Saul Friedlander, eds. *Les Juifs et le XXe siècle*, Paris: Calmann-Lévy, 2000, p. 228.

4. Joseph Massad, "Antisemitism, the highest stage of Zionism," *Middle East Eye,* June 15, 2023.
5. Alan MacLeod, "The Israel Files: Wikileaks docs show top Hollywood producers working with Israel to defend its war crimes," *Mintpress News*, September 23, 2022.
6. Quoted in: Shlaim 2025, *op. cit.*, p. 312.
7. Joe Biden, Biden in 2007 interview: I am a Zionist, *Shalom TV,* April 2007.
8. John Mearsheimer, "The Israel Lobby is as Powerful as Ever," *New Statesman,* February 10, 2024.
9. "Settlement champion Huckabee confirmed as US Israel envoy," *English Alarabiya*, April 10, 2025.
10. Richard Connor *et. al.*, "Germany's Merz says Israel doing 'dirty work for us' in Iran," *Deutsche Welle*, June 17, 2025.
11. Itamar Eichner, "Putin's surprising reason for not providing war aid to Iran: 'Israel is almost a Russian-speaking country,'" *Ynet Global,* June 21, 2025.
12. "'A Hideous Atrocity': Noam Chomsky on Israel's Assault on Gaza & U.S. Support for the Occupation," *Democracy Now,* August 7, 2014.

Critics

1. Elhanan Bunim Wasserman, *The Epoch of the Messiah*, Brooklyn, NY: Ohr Elchonon, 1976, pp. 17-30.
2. "Rabbi Yosef Tzvi Dushinsky, Chief Rabbi of Jerusalem (1867-1948)" *Torah Jews* website.
3. "May Jews Wage War or Battles in Our Time?" *Jewish Guardian*, vol. 2, no. 8, Spring 1984.
4. David Yehudiof, *Hasabba Kadisha Baba Salé* [the Holy Old Man Baba Salé], vol. 2, Netivot, Israel: Barukh Abuhatsera, 1987, pp. 217–19.
5. Allan C. Brownfeld, "Zionism at 100: Remembering Its Often Prophetic Jewish Critics," *Issues, American Council for Judaism*, Summer 1997.

6. *Ibid.*, p. 9.
7. Idan Zonshine, "Iran's Chief Rabbi Says Zionists 'Do Not Represent Judaism," *Jerusalem Post,* May 27, 2020.
8. "Memorandum of Edwin Montagu on the Anti-Semitism of the Present (British) Government - Submitted to the British Cabinet, August 1917," at jewishvirtuallibrary.org.
9. Uri Misgav, "Not neo-Nazis, Judeo-Nazis," *Haaretz* May 30, 2014.
10. https://sites.google.com/site/jewsagainstracistzionism/blum.
11. Machover, *op. cit.*
12. Nissim Ahmed, "Desmond Tutu: 'Israeli Apartheid worse than South Africa,'" *Middle East Monitor*, October 7, 2024.
13. https://www.youtube.com/watch?v=S6DznZTgoDc&ab_channel=JudgeNapolitano-JudgingFreedom.
14. Orly Noy, "Israel is waging a holocaust in Gaza. Denazification is our only remedy." *+972 Magazine,* September 18, 2025.

TRACTION

Current and forthcoming titles from TRACTION

1. **ZIONISM DECODED IN 101 QUOTES**
   By Yakov Rabkin
2. **RWANDA'S 30-YEAR ASSAULT ON CONGO**
   The Crimes, The Criminals and the Cover-up
   by Judi Rever
3. **LAST CALL FOR CANADA**
   Sovereign Nation or Vassal State
   by Peter McFarlane
4. **NUMB**
   The Politics of Overwhelm
   by Mark Abley

Printed by Imprimerie Gauvin
Gatineau, Québec